CRAFTSMAN'S · GUIDES

RE-UPHOLSTERY TECHNIQUES

Derek Balfour

Little, Brown and Company
Boston   Toronto

To Allanah Campbell, Gerald, Tessa, Jarvis and Lesley

Library of Congress catalog card no 85-82358

First American edition

Conceived and produced by
Swallow Publishing Limited, London

Editor: Anne Yelland
Art director: Glynis Edwards
Designer: Barry Walsh
Illustrators: Steve Cross, Hussein Hussein, Aziz Khan, Coral Mula, Rob Shone
Photography: Jon Bouchier
Studio: Barry Walsh
Picture research: Liz Eddison

Acknowledgements

Swallow Books gratefully acknowledge the assistance given to them in the production of *Re-upholstery Techniques* by the following people and organizations. We apologize to anyone we may have omitted to mention.

Photographs: Derek Balfour 4, 35, 48, 62(I), 65(B); Jon Bouchier 1, 6, 8, 10, 13(R), 14, 16, 22, 24, 29, 31, 32, 37, 45, 47, 62(FP), 65(T), 69, 72, 73, 75; The Bridgeman Art Library 13(L); Eldridge, London 71(B); Jeremy Mulcaire 52, 57, 61; Elizabeth Whiting and Associates 71(T) – photographer Tom Leighton.
(I) – Inset; (B) – Bottom; (R) – Right; (FP) – Full Page; (T) – Top.

Fabrics on pages 72/73 supplied by Sanderson.
Braids on page 75 supplied by T.A. Hodder and Co Ltd.

Re-upholstery on pages 1, 4, 16, 22, 24, 28, 31, 32, 35, 37, 45, 47, 48, 62, 69 by Derek Balfour. Pages 52, 57, 61 by Joan Ball.

Illustrations: Steve Cross 34, 35, 44, 60, 75, 76; Hussein Hussein 13, 27, 28, 30, 69; Aziz Khan 18, 21, 23, 36, 39, 40, 43, 49, 50, 54, 55, 57, 59; Coral Mula 15; Rob Shone 61, 67.

We are grateful to the London College of Furniture for their assistance in the preparation of this book.

Published simultaneously in Canada
by Little, Brown & Company (Canada) Limited

Printed in Italy

Contents

Introduction   4

Tools and equipment   6

Materials used in traditional upholstery   8

Basic construction   12

Chair frames   14

Project 1: Drop-in seat   16

Project 2: Stuffed and stitched
   dining-chair seat   24

Project 3: Wing armchair, with sprung
   seat and back, and scroll arms   32

Project 4: Sofa with cushioned seat   52

Project 5: Nineteenth-century
   button-back nursing chair   62

Fabrics for upholstery   72

Upholstery trimmings   74

Introduction

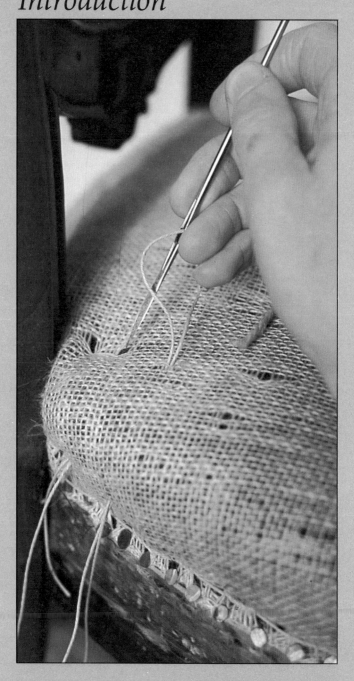

Brief history

Upholstered furniture, in its broadest sense, is any furniture to which material – leather or some sort of textile – is fixed. From decorations in tombs, we know that some form of upholstered furniture existed in ancient Egypt. In Europe, however, it seems that upholstery was restricted to simple cushions for a very long time.

The stuffed and stitched constructions which we call 'traditional' developed in the eighteenth century and did not change very much until the introduction of springs about a hundred years later. In England, springs were patented by Samuel Pratt in 1828 but had possibly been used in France in the late eighteenth century. Many filling materials have been used over the years but feathers and horse and cattle hair seem to date back to the earliest upholstery.

Re-upholstery

This book has been set out in projects, each more complicated than the last. The pieces have been chosen to cover as many techniques and constructions as possible so that with thought and careful note-taking you can tackle other items not covered here. If you are about to begin your first piece of upholstery do not attempt an armchair; you may lose heart simply by the length of time it takes. To give some idea of the time involved, the first project may take almost a whole day, and the second could take you two or three days.

Read the projects right through several times before you start work so that you have some understanding of what you are aiming for. Remember that you are in charge and can take out something you do not like – such as a row of stitching – and begin again; aim for perfection but do not give up if your first attempts are not too good. It is a good plan to do several similar items one after another before you move on to more complicated work. No matter how tempted you may be to start work on your grandmother's button-back chair, wait until you know you can solve the problems you may come across.

Left: *One of the techniques which is basic to traditional upholstery is forming rows of stitching to make a firm edge. The upholstery will then hold its shape for many years.*

Tools and equipment

For consistency, throughout we have given sizes and measurements in metric, with their imperial equivalents in brackets. Many of these items, however, are sold in standard imperial measures.

Upholsterer's hammers are available with various different combinations of face, but you should have one with one plain face, about 12mm (½in.) in diameter. It does not matter if the other end has a claw or is magnetic.

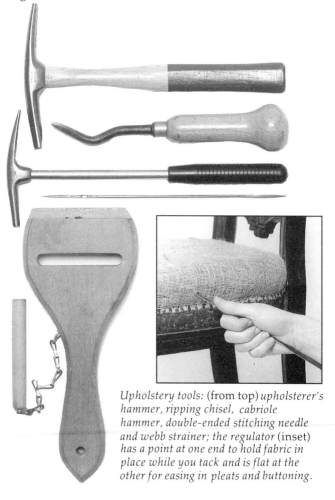

Upholstery tools: (from top) *upholsterer's hammer, ripping chisel, cabriole hammer, double-ended stitching needle and webb strainer; the regulator* (inset) *has a point at one end to hold fabric in place while you tack and is flat at the other for easing in pleats and buttoning.*

The cabriole hammer has an extra small face, about 8mm (5⁄16in.) in diameter, and is useful when you are tacking close to polished show-wood or carving.

A ripping chisel is essential, inexpensive and used for ripping out old upholstery. It looks rather like a screwdriver with a hardened edge to the blade, and is available with either a cranked or straight shaft.

The webb strainer enables you to pull webbing more tightly than would otherwise be possible. The 'bat' type is the most common and inexpensive.

A regulator is used mainly for moving the stuffing about within the scrim ('regulating') and is essential. Of the various lengths and gauges, 23 or 25cm (9 or 10in.) and a fairly light gauge is the most useful.

Buttoning and stitching needles are double-ended. There are two types, round-pointed for buttoning work and bayonet- (triangular) pointed for stitching. They are available in various lengths and gauges, but 25cm (10in.) and fairly heavy gauge is best to begin with.

The spring needle is a curved needle with a flattened point used for stitching springs to webbing and inserting bridle ties.

Semi-circular needles are available in various sizes and gauges from 25mm (1in.) to 15cm (6in.). The smaller sizes are used for slip-stitching, the larger ones where it would be difficult to use a straight needle.

A wooden mallet is used with the ripping chisel for removing old tacks and upholstery, so it should be fairly large.

Shears should be good quality and stay sharp right to the points for snipping. Any good scissors can be used, but 20 or 23cm (8 or 9in.) is the most useful size.

Upholstery skewers (pins) are often used to hold hessian (burlap), scrim or the top cover in place.

Steel pins hold fabric in place while you work. The most practical are 40mm (1½in.) long adamantine pins.

A table for working on. Upholsterers use a trestle table but a table top alone is satisfactory for most jobs.

Other tools which may be useful include a sharp craft knife; pliers; tailor's chalk; a soft tape measure and a straight length of wood for cutting piping, etc.

Materials used in traditional upholstery

Hessian (burlap) is made from jute and is available in three weights:

340g (12oz.) is used over webbing and/or springs as the base on which all the upholstery is constructed;

280g (10oz.) is used in much the same way as 340g (12oz.);

210g (7½oz.) is sometimes used instead of scrim to enclose the first stuffing.

Scrim is used to enclose the first stuffing. Like hessian, it is usually made from jute but the yarn used is finer spun. Linen scrim may be used on high-grade work.

The weight of both hessian and scrim relates to a piece of material 115cm × 90cm (45in. × 36in.).

Calico (muslin) is used under the top cover to enclose all the fillings. Either medium- or lightweight is the most suitable for upholstery.

Cambric is closely woven and waxed cotton used to make the inner feather-filled cases of cushions.

Bottoming, which is also sometimes called upholsterer's linen (though now usually made from cotton), is used for the base of chairs and catches any dust which falls from the filling.

Webbing is used as a support for all the other fillings. It can be either plain woven jute or twill woven cotton and flax (which is often termed English webbing). Both types are usually about 5cm (2in.) wide, jute webbing comes in rolls of 33m (36yds) and English webbing in rolls of 16.5m (18yds).

Linter felt, which is also known as cotton felt, is made from fine cotton fibres, and produced as a thick padding in rolls about 66cm (26in.) wide. It is used over the second stuffing but under the top cover.

Skin wadding (batting) is a very thin layer of wadding made of cotton with a 'skin' sprayed on to hold the fibres together. It is used in the same way as linter felt but on small chairs.

Left to right: *hessian, used as a base; scrim, to encase stuffing; calico, an undercovering; cambric, for cushion cases; bottoming, for catching dust; linter felt and skin wadding, for padding under the top cover; and herringbone webbing.*

Coir fibre.   Curled hair.

Curled hair, although referred to as horse hair, is today mostly a mixture of horse and hog hair. The best grade is still pure horse and should be long, stranded and very curly. Hair found in chairs can often be washed and reused. It is generally used as a second stuffing only today because of its high cost.

Fibre is a substitute for hair. Coir fibre (made from the husk of the coconut) is the most common today although hay, reeds and seaweed have all been used in the past. Coir is available either as a ginger fibre or dyed black; the latter is easier to work with but it does tend to stain the hands. Fibre should not be reused.

Upholstery tacks, also termed 'blued' cut tacks, have fine sharp points. There are two types: improved and fine. Improved have rather large heads and thick

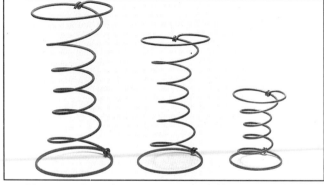

Double-cone or hourglass springs are available in various heights and wire thicknesses.

shanks, fine, as their name implies, have small heads and thin shanks. Tacks are available in various lengths but three are usual in upholstery:

15mm (⅝in.) are used for fixing webbing. The thickness of the timber dictates whether to use improved or fine, since a fine tack is less likely to split hard timber than the thicker improved tack;

12mm (½in.) are used for fixing webbing on light frames, such as you would find with a drop-in seat or delicate pin-stuffed work. Fine are used for temporary tacking hessian and scrim and fixing base hessian;

10mm (⅜in.) improved are used for fixing hessian and scrim, fine are used for fixing calico and top covers.

Gimp pins are mainly used for fixing gimp but are also useful for fixing the top cover on a fragile chair or in places where a tack would look unsightly. They are available in many colours.

Twine for use in upholstery is usually made of hemp and either jute or flax. There are three thicknesses: stout for sewing in springs and similar heavy work; medium for stitching edges; and fine for buttoning and for bridle ties. Nylon twine is now often used for buttoning work. Twine is available in 250g (8oz.) balls.

Laid cord is usually made of hemp, and its strands are laid together so that they do not stretch. Used for lashing (cording) springs, it is sold in 500g (17oz.) balls.

Piping cord (welting) is made of three-stranded soft cotton and sold by number (00,1,2,3, etc.). The lower the number the finer the cord, although thicknesses tend to vary from manufacturer to manufacturer. Pile fabrics may need finer cord than non-pile fabrics.

Slipping (buttoning) thread is used to hand-stitch top covers. Any good carpet thread is suitable if you cannot get upholsterer's linen thread. The thread is available in various colours, but natural is the most useful.

Springs used in traditional upholstery are termed double-cone or hourglass springs because of their shape. They are available in varying heights from 75mm (3in.) to 35cm (14in.) and wire thicknesses (SWG – standard wire gauge/metal diameter) from 8 to 15. Gauges 9 and 10 are used for seats (10 is the most useful); 11, 12 and 13 for backs and 14 and 15 for arms. Other types of springing are not covered in the projects in this book.

Basic construction

Traditional upholstery consists of layers of varying thickness of woven and loose materials. The number of layers varies, but they are always built up in the same way. Webbing tacked to the frame takes most of the strain and supports the springs, if there are any. Some chairs are unsprung, others can have them in the seat, back and arms. Both the height and the thickness (swg/metal diameter) of springs vary, but they are always attached to the webbing in the same way. The springs are then lashed (corded) together so that they move together to some extent.

A covering of strong hessian (burlap) is placed over the webbing or springs and the springs are attached to this in the same way as they were to the webbing. This forms a base for the first stuffing. This first stuffing is a loose material, either hair or (more usually, these days) fibre, and is anchored to the hessian by means of twine ties. Scrim encloses the first stuffing.

If the outer edge of the part being upholstered is of any height, a hard edge (edge roll) is constructed so that it holds its shape. A hard edge can be made on a straight or curved edge and on a seat, back, arm or wing, though not necessarily every edge on the same piece of furniture will have a hard edge. There are many ways of making an edge firm and able to retain its shape, but the one most often used is produced by forming rows of stitching with twine along the edge to hold the filling in place in the edge. One or more rows of blind (sink) stitches pull fibre into the base of the seat, and one or more rows of top stitches hold the edge firm. Other methods of constructing edges have been used over the centuries, but this is the most common among traditional upholstery craftsmen.

A second layer of stuffing, this time thin and unstitched, covers the scrim; this stuffing should be hair, and is held in place by calico (muslin). The calico also helps to create the final shape of the piece. A layer of wadding (batting) over the calico helps stop the hair filling working its way through the calico and sticking through the top cover.

Many different fabrics can be used for the top cover, but advice on choosing the most suitable is given on pp. 72-3.

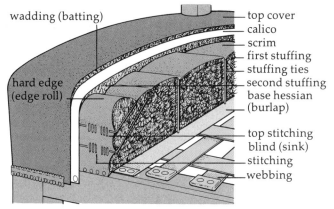

wadding (batting)
hard edge (edge roll)

top cover
calico
scrim
first stuffing
stuffing ties
second stuffing
base hessian (burlap)
top stitching
blind (sink) stitching
webbing

Cross-section of an unsprung chair.

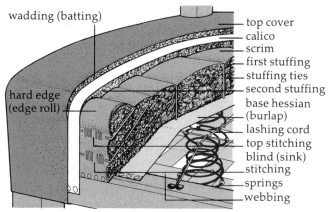

wadding (batting)
hard edge (edge roll)

top cover
calico
scrim
first stuffing
stuffing ties
second stuffing
base hessian (burlap)
lashing cord
top stitching
blind (sink) stitching
springs
webbing

Cross-section of a sprung chair.

Although springs make a chair more comfortable, there is little difference in the basic construction techniques.

Chair frames

Most traditional frames are made of wood, usually beech or birch, and there are two basic frame types: stuffover, which are completely upholstered (excluding the legs) and show-wood, in which the wood, sometimes with decorative carving, is left exposed. The visible part of the frame can be made from any wood.

The joints used on the chair will depend on the quality and date of the piece. It will usually have dowelled or mortise and tenon joints or a combination of both. Although each part of the frame has a (usually obvious) name, all stuffover frames have one set of rails which are vital to the upholsterer; these are the stay or stuffing rails. These rails form a space at about seat height through which the covers pass.

Many modern frames (even of traditional style) are termed 'knock down' because the arms, back and seat are upholstered as separate units, which are then bolted together before the outside cover is attached. These frames, and iron-frame chairs, are not dealt with here.

stay or stuffing rails

Most chair frames are simple and often look too fragile to hold the upholstery; the stay or stuffing rails are vital in re-upholstery.

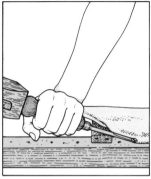

Stripping old upholstery

Use the ripping chisel and a mallet to strip the old upholstery off the frame. Work along the grain of the wood.

Stripping frames

If your chair is of some value or of a genuinely early date, consult a professional or your local museum before you do anything, even before you strip the upholstery off. Before you remove anything from the frame, make sketches or take photographs from all sides of the chair. Note things like the height of the seat at the edge, where the piping is and the size and shape at the front of the arms. You may think you will remember, but once the chair is stripped it will be too late to find out that you cannot. Begin by stripping the bottoming off the chair with the ripping chisel and the mallet. Work along the grain of the wood away from the corners, being careful not to split the wood. Next, remove the outside back and outside arms, making more notes and sketches as you go. You will need to know, for example, if the inside arm goes out through the back of the chair, or through the side of the arm close to the back. As you take the chair apart, look at the illustrations in the book which look similar; it may help you later.

When you have removed all the upholstery and tacks, look at the joints. If they are loose, reglue them. If the tacking area looks as though you may have difficulty anchoring the tacks in place, mix sawdust with a little wood glue and fill the holes. Glue strips of either hessian or calico over these areas to help hold the sawdust filling in place. If the polished show-wood needs repairing, get advice from a professional restorer.

Project 1: Drop-in seat

Simple seats

The upholstery in drop-in seats is simple and dates from about the seventeenth century, when the backs of chairs were sometimes constructed in the same way.

The frame to which the upholstery is fixed is usually made up of four battens of wood (usually beech) jointed at the corners. Some are serpentine-shaped along the front edge, but this makes very little difference to the way the upholstery is built up. The subframe sits in the main chair frame with a space between them – this is the space into which the covering fabrics fit.

Although, as a general rule, the edges of drop-in seats are not visible, sometimes the front and back edges are and the front edge is rounded off instead of flat. In this case, you must take care that both of these edges are very neat and that the undercovering does not show below the edge of the seat.

In spite of their simple construction, drop-in seats are not very easy to work on, simply because they move about easily. When you are fixing the webbing, either clamp the frame to the bench or tack a strip of old webbing to the bench across one corner of the frame – this will stop the frame from lifting up when you tension the webbing. When you strip the frame, note how many webbs there are in each direction. In almost all cases the old upholstery of a drop-in seat should be removed and discarded. The padding tends to flatten and the webbing stretch, and the result is a hollow seat.

Basic techniques

A drop-in seat is a good project to begin with because it involves many of the basic techniques of upholstery. Although there are variations from one piece to another, the application of these techniques and the method of working are the same whether you are dealing with a seat, back, arm or wing.

If you have more than one drop-in seat to re-upholster, work on two at a time so that they will look about the same when you have finished.

Left: Re-upholstering a drop-in seat is a good project to start with because it is quite simple and relatively quick, but also involves many of the basic techniques of upholstery: the fixing of webbing and hessian; making bridle ties to anchor the filling; and fitting calico, skin wadding and top and bottom covers.

Webbing

Webbing is usually fixed to the top of the frame in unsprung chairs and the bottom of the frame in sprung chairs. The top outer edge of a drop-in seat should be chamfered (beveled), so if your seat does not have a chamfered edge, you should put one on first. The webbing must be spaced evenly over the area formed by the seat rails, so start by marking the centre of all four rails on both the top and bottom surfaces.

Always work from a roll of webbing; you will have problems if you start cutting lengths off the roll to work with. Fold 2.5cm (1in.) of the cut end of the webbing over on itself. Line up the webbing at the centre back of

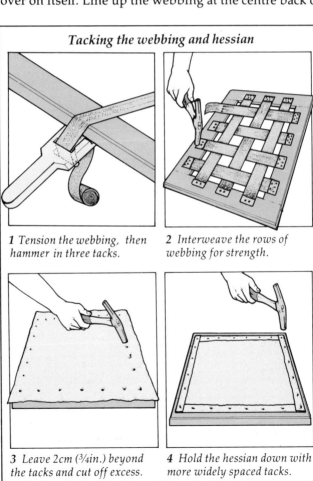

Tacking the webbing and hessian

1 Tension the webbing, then hammer in three tacks.

2 Interweave the rows of webbing for strength.

3 Leave 2cm (¾in.) beyond the tacks and cut off excess.

4 Hold the hessian down with more widely spaced tacks.

the frame, with the fold about halfway across the width of the frame and hammer in five tacks in a W shape. Unless the wood is hard and liable to split (in which case you should use 12mm (½in.) fine), use 12mm (½in.) improved tacks. The cut end of the webbing should be on top (thus forming a 'washer' under the tack head). Thread the webb strainer and tension the webbing towards the front of the frame. Overstraining will warp a light frame but the webbing should still be drum-like, not saggy. Line up the webbing at the centre front and, again halfway across the rail, drive three tacks fully home into the single thickness of webbing while you are straining it. Cut the webbing about 2.5cm (1in.) from the tacks and fold this back on itself, then hammer in two more tacks. If you could see all five tacks at this end, they would make the same W shape. The number of rows of webbing you removed when you were stripping the chair is the best guide to how many rows you will need. Work outwards from the centre back and do all the back to front rows, then do the side to side rows, interweaving them.

Base hessian (burlap)

The base hessian covers the webbing and supports the filling, so if it sags, the filling will too. Measure across the widest part of the frame (side to side and front to back) and add about 5cm (2in.) on each edge for handling and turning over, then cut a piece of hessian to these measurements. Fold it in half, front to back and mark the centre then place it over the webbing, keeping the weave square to the seat. The hessian can then be temporary tacked. This involves driving the tacks only part way into the wood, so that they can be removed easily if adjustments have to be made. Use 10mm (⅜in.) improved tacks and start at the centre of the back rail. Strain the hessian to the centre front and temporary tack it there, then repeat at each side. Continue temporary tacking on the back rail, spacing the tacks about 4cm (1½in.) apart, then do the front edge, tensioning the hessian as you work, and then do the sides. When the whole frame is temporary tacked, hammer the tacks on the front rail home. As you do the back rail, tension the hessian slightly and when you hammer home on the side rails, keep checking that the weave is square.

Finish the edges as illustrated opposite.

Filling the seat

Bridle ties are made with a spring needle and thin twine. Start about 6.5cm (2½in.) from the edge of the frame, knot the twine, then make a looped running stitch around the seat, only knotting the twine again at the end of the run. The centre section will need some ties, though how many depends on size – for a small seat, one single loop down the centre is enough. The height of the loops varies according to how much filling you need; for a drop-in seat they need only be high enough to allow your hand to slide under them.

The best filling for a small area like a drop-in seat is hair. This is easy to handle and, unlike other fillings which go flat after only a short time, is resilient. To avoid lumps, tease the hair before you use it. To do this, take a handful and pull the fibres apart, letting them drop into a plastic bag. When you have a reasonable amount teased, take a handful and, starting at the back left-hand corner, tuck it under the bridle ties. As you tuck in each successive handful, tease it into the rest of the hair. Do all the sides of the seat first, then fill in the centre section. You should put slightly more here.

Covering with calico (muslin)

Measure over the filling at its widest point and round to the bottom of the frame and add about 5cm (2in.) on all sides for handling, before you cut the calico. The weave must be kept square at all times, so fold the material and mark its centre. If the space between the seat and the chair frame is not large enough to take the thickness of the tack head, calico and top cover, tack the calico to the underside of the seat. Normally, it should be tacked to the outer face of the frame. Using 10mm (⅜in.) fine tacks, temporary tack at the centres of the back, front and sides, keeping the calico square and quite taut. Place more tacks about 4cm (1½in.) apart along the back rail, then tension the calico towards the front rail and tack it there. Finally, temporary tack the sides. Take care that the filling does not slip on to the face edge of the frame at any point.

If, when you have finished, the shape is not quite right, take out a few tacks at a time and tension and shape again smoothing it over the edges and towards the corners. Finish the corners as shown opposite. Finally, tack home all around the sides.

Filling a drop-in seat

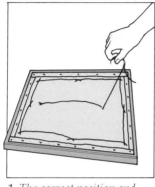

1 *The correct position and height of bridle ties.*

2 *Teased hair will give a lump- and hollow-free filling.*

3 *As you work, tension the calico to make the right shape.*

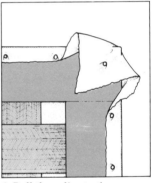

4 *Pull the calico to the corner; tack with a gimp pin.*

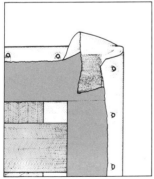

5 *Pleat the first side, tack home and cut away excess.*

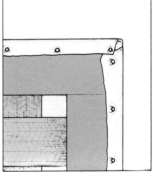

6 *Pleat the second side over the first and tack home.*

Skin wadding (batting)

Skin wadding is essential with a hair filling and is used on top of the calico to prevent the filling working through the top cover. It also adds softness to the surface covering. Cut a piece of wadding to cover the seat easily, then, holding it in place over the calico, pinch away any excess as far down as the top of the seat rail. This will prevent a hard edge showing on the top cover, which would happen if the wadding were cut. Take care that the wadding does not cover the face edges of the frame; if it does, you will find it difficult to fit the seat back into the frame.

Top and bottom covers

If the fabric you have chosen for the top cover has a pattern, remember when you are cutting out that you must centre the pattern. Tack the cover to the underside of the frame with 10mm (⅜in.) fine tacks. Space them as you did for the calico, about 10mm (⅜in.) in from outer edge, and, as with the calico, temporary tack first so that you can check the fit as you go. At the corners, fold the material to make pleats on the front and back edges.

Although the frame of this seat was not in perfect condition (left), the finished upholstery (right) should last for many years.

Fitting the cover

1 Pinch away excess wadding to prevent a hard edge.

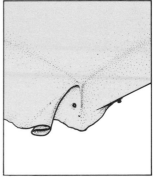

2 Ease fabric to the back edge and fix with a gimp pin.

3 Pleat the fabric, cut away excess and tack home.

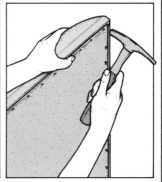

4 Tack one edge of the bottoming under the other.

Use gimp pins at the corners since they reduce bulk, and then cut off any excess.

The final stage is to fix the bottom cover, which catches any dust falling from the seat and also covers all the raw edges of the top cover. Although bottoming is usually black, you can use any close-weave fabric like curtain lining. Cut a rectangle of bottoming the same size as the base of the frame and temporary tack using 10mm (⅜in.) fine tacks, folding it under as you go. The fold should be about 10mm (⅜in.) from the edge of the frame, and the bottoming pulled just tight enough not to sag. Tack close to the fold so that the edge lies flat and space the tacks about 2.5cm (1in.) apart. This time, fold the corners one under the other.

Project 2: Stuffed and stitched dining-chair seat

Basic construction

There are several differences between a drop-in seat and this type of dining-chair seat. The first is that the upholstery is attached directly to the chair frame instead of to a subframe. Secondly, the filling here is much thicker than in a drop-in seat and therefore some way of keeping the shape of the stuffing has to be found. The stuffing in the drop-in seat was covered with calico (muslin) to create the seat shape; in the dining-chair, the shape is created by encasing the filling in scrim which is tacked to the edge of the seat frame – the top of the outer edge of the seat rail should be chamfered (beveled) for this purpose. Rows of stitching formed with twine are then inserted through the scrim and the filling to form a firm edge so that the seat keeps its shape even after many years' use. The stuffing, tacking and stitching described here constitute the basic and most often used method of creating an edge in traditional upholstery.

A further difference is that the drop-in seat had only one filling, while this seat has two. The filling over the hessian is called the first stuffing, the next (much thinner) filling is called the second stuffing. This is covered with calico, as in the drop-in seat.

Most chairs of this type are finished off on the lower edge by gimp or braid. Choose a gimp which is a suitable width in proportion to the depth of the upholstery – wide gimp or braid will tend to dominate a shallow seat. Always follow the line of the show-wood when you are fixing gimp.

Preparation

When you strip the chair, note how the corners are finished. Are there two pleats or one, for example? Note how high the seat is and where it comes to on the back posts, this will be a guide later when you build the seat. Measure the height of the front too.

If you have two or more chairs which are meant to be identical then work on them both at the same time; it will be easier to make them look the same this way.

Finally, before you start, remember to reglue the frame, if necessary (see p. 15).

Left: *From worn and collapsed* (top) *to firm and comfortable. The seat of this dining chair is stitched so that it holds its shape.*

First stages

Attach the webbing, as described on pp. 18-19. Use 340g (12oz.) hessian (burlap) as a base over the webbing. Fix it as described on pp. 18-19, but at the corners, tack it on top of the front legs, and cut it to fit around the back posts. Insert bridle ties as described on pp. 20-1 but here allow about three fingers' height. Although hair is preferred as a stuffing where only a thin padding is needed, fibre is acceptable as a first stuffing for most other work, so use that here. Tease and insert it in the same way as described for hair on pp. 20-1.

Allow enough scrim to cover the filling and come down to the bottom of the seat rails. Fold the scrim to find the centre, and, keeping the weave straight, temporary tack it at the back, then smooth it to the front and temporary tack it there. Tack both sides. Be careful not to put the tacks into any show-wood.

Stuffing ties

Use a regulator or chalk to mark the position of the ties, which should run round the seat about 10cm (4in.) from the edge of the seat rail. Thread the stitching needle with no. 2 twine and, in the back left-hand corner (A), stab down through the scrim, stuffing and base hessian. Insert the needle in the hessian 12mm (½in.) along and push up and out through the scrim on top–the needle should come out 12mm (½in.) from where you stabbed down originally–and form a slip knot. Stab down again at B and come back up again. Continue doing this until you have a running stitch around the seat. Pull each stitch firm but not tight and then loosely tie off the twine at A. Then put a couple of ties down the centre of the seat to secure the filling there.

Once the stuffing ties are in position, the scrim can be turned under and tacked on to the chamfered edge. Remove the temporary tacks at the centre front. You will need to add more fibre to make the edge firm, so tease out a handful, lift the scrim and push the new fibre *under* the existing fibre mass. Work round the seat in this way, removing tacks from a section at a time, then fold the scrim under the filling (the regulator will help considerably here), and tack it on the chamfered edge using 12mm (½in.) fine tacks, about 10mm (⅜in.) apart. When you have tacked about 40mm (1½in.) either side of the centre, measure the height of the seat

Enclosing the first stuffing

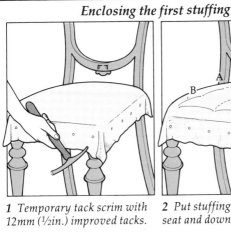

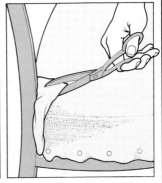

1 *Temporary tack scrim with 12mm (½in.) improved tacks.*

2 *Put stuffing ties around the seat and down the centre.*

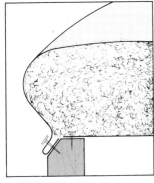

3 *Scrim turned under and tacked on the chamfered edge.*

4 *Cut towards the corner post, but stop 15mm (⅝in.) short.*

from the floor. Keep measuring from the floor as you work round and if your edge is too high at any point, remove the tacks and fold more scrim under the filling (if there is a lot of scrim to turn under, cut some away); this will lower the edge, but it must still protrude beyond the edge of the seat rail. Follow the shape of the seat rails and tack along the front, then the back, then each side, to within 50mm (2in.) of each corner.

At the back corners, fold the scrim back on itself, and make a cut. Tuck the scrim down between the back post and the stuffing, make a fold inwards, cut any excess off the bottom of the scrim and tack it. At the front corners, pleat the scrim, cut off any excess at the bottom, then turn it under and tack. Hammer all the tacks home.

Making a hard edge (edge roll)

The most common way of making a hard edge is by stitching: a blind (sink) stitch pulls fibre into the base of the seat, while a top stitch holds the edge firm. It is usual for this type of seat to have one blind row and two top rows of stitching. To make the blind stitch, thread the stitching needle with stitching (buttoning) twine, and starting in the back left-hand corner, insert the needle through the side of the scrim, close to the post and the tacks. The point should come out through the top of the seat about 70mm (2¾in.) from the edge. Do not pull the needle free (the eye should come to the top surface of the scrim). Make a circular motion with the

Blind (sink) stitching

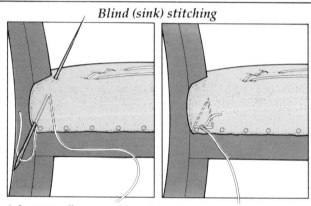

1 *Insert needle, eye end last, through the scrim. Make a circular motion with the end, push needle back down, make a slip knot.*

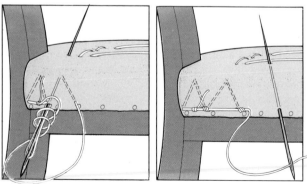

2 *After the next stitch, loop left-hand twine round needle twice, withdraw the needle and pull the twine downwards.*

The stitched edge forms the shape of the finished seat.

eye end and push the needle down so that it comes out of the scrim near where you first inserted it. Take the needle out and make a slip knot. Tighten the twine gently but firmly. Insert the needle about 20mm (¾in.) along from the slip knot and make another stitch as before, but do not withdraw the needle this time. Loop the twine round the needle twice, withdraw the needle and pull the twine downwards. Work around the seat in this way, then work the back in exactly the same way.

Regulate the fibre into the edge of the seat, and keep regulating as you work around the seat. The rows of stitching must be evenly spaced up the height of the seat and about 12mm (½in.) apart. Insert the needle (eye end last) and stab upwards, coming out on the top surface a little way in from the edge. Pull the needle clear of the scrim, then push it down near to the back post. Pull it clear of the seat and form a slip knot. Insert the needle again about 20mm (¾in.) from the first stitch, come out on the top surface as before, stab down alongside the first stitch, then loop the twine twice around the needle, withdraw the needle, and pull the stitch tight. Work round the seat in this way, then work the back edge. Thread all the loose ends of twine up into the seat and tighten and tie off the stuffing ties.

The second stuffing should be a fairly thin layer of hair, inserted as described on pp. 20-1. When you have finished, the surface of the chair should feel springy and the centre of the seat should dome slightly.

Calico and wadding (batting)

Cut a rectangle of calico to cover the seat at its widest
point and come down to the bottom of the seat rail. The
weave must be kept square on top of the seat, so fold or
mark the centre line so that you can see it easily.
Temporary tack the back using 10mm (⅜in.) fine tacks,
then smooth and strain the calico to the front. Repeat at
each side. The calico must be quite tight and tacked
halfway down the seat rail, to within 50mm (2in.) of
each corner. Finish the back corners as illustrated
below. Use the flat end of the regulator to ease the calico
between the stuffing and the post. If it puckers near the
post, you will have to lift it and lengthen the cut a little.

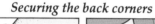

Securing the back corners

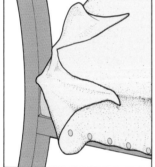

1 *Slash the calico to within
6mm (¼in.) of the post.*

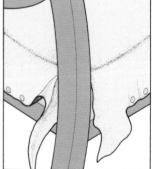

2 *Ease it down between the
post and the filling.*

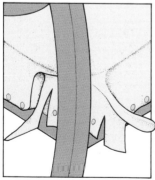

3 *Tack almost on chamfered
edge and cut near the tack.*

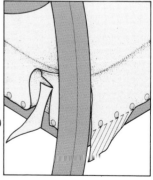

4 *Fold it to come to the post,
and cut off any excess.*

Find the centre of the front corners, strain the calico to that point, and fix it with a gimp pin. Tack that home. Put a pin each side of the corner, smooth the calico down and pleat it inwards. Use the flat end of the regulator to get a good fold line. Ease the calico into place, drive all the tacks home and trim off any excess.

Cut a piece of skin wadding to fit over the seat and cover the tacks, and trim away any excess by pinching as described on pp. 22-3. Cut it to fit around the corner posts, easing down between the post and the seat.

Top and bottom covers

Measure for the top cover as you did for the calico, but remember that any pattern must be centred. The top cover must finish at the show-wood, so make sure that any gimp or braid you use will cover the tacks as you place them. Use 10mm (⅜in.) fine tacks and temporary tack first at the back, then smooth and strain to the front. Repeat at the sides, constantly checking that the cover remains straight and quite tight. Fix the corners as you did the calico, but remember that the tacks must not be visible when the gimp is applied. When you are satisfied that all is square and neat, hammer the tacks home, being careful not to damage the show-wood. Trim away excess fabric using a sharp knife or scissors.

Although gimp should be attached with matching gimp pins, gluing with a clear adhesive is easier. Do not use too much glue, which could bleed through the gimp and discolour it. Follow the show-wood line, and try not to stretch the gimp. The corners should be mitred.

Fit a bottom cover as described on pp. 22-3.

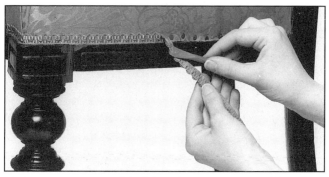

As long as you are careful, gluing gimp is quite acceptable and easier than attaching it with gimp pins.

Project 3: Wing armchair, with sprung seat and back, and scroll arms

Basic construction

The major difference between this project and the previous ones is that here the parts of the chair have to be upholstered so that they meet each other without gaps. Gaps look dreadful and adding bits of wadding (batting) when the top cover is partly fitted makes matters worse. The stay or stuffing rails are vital here – their position indicates the height of the seat.

The seat is usually the first part of a chair to fail. The webbing decays naturally and pulls away from the tacks and the base hessian (burlap) also sometimes rots with the result that the filling is pushed down into the spring area. The tops of the arms tend to lose their resilience and become dented where the elbows are rested. The back is usually the last to go. For this reason, it is not always necessary to strip all the upholstery off a chair but even if you can salvage the back and wings, the seat and arms should be stripped to the frame.

If you are in any doubt about how long the old upholstery will last if you leave it, remember that the covering material is the most expensive part of the job, except for your time, and that it will be better in the long run to start from scratch than to risk the chair collapsing after only perhaps a year or two.

Preparation

When you are stripping the chair, make drawings and notes of what sort of finish it has. Is there any piping (welting), if so where and how is it fixed? Where do the facings fit and what shape are they? It is not essential that you reproduce the original exactly, but it will be useful as a guide.

It is usually easier to webb, spring and base hessian the seat and back first, while the frame is free from upholstery, then begin stuffing the chair. Do the first stuffing of the whole chair, then the second stuffing and calico (muslin) of the whole chair, and finally the wadding and top cover. When a piece of furniture has identical sections such as arms and, as here, wings, work each stage of these sections at the same time; this will help you to make them match.

Left: *The seat of this chair had fallen out* (far left) *and extensive work had to be done on the frame; nothing could be reused. Most chairs look completely different when they are finished* (top).

Sprung seat

In unsprung work, the webbing is tacked on the top of the seat frame. In most sprung seats, however, it is fixed to the underside. With this exception, you should attach the webbing as described on pp. 18-19. Use 15mm (⅝in.) improved tacks and be particularly careful that you tack the webbing halfway across the rail; if it is too close to the outside edge of the frame, it will show as ugly bumps under the top cover.

Check the notes you made when you were stripping the chair to see how deep the back and arms were. It is pointless to put springs too close to the back rail if they are going to be covered by the stuffing (filling) in the chair back, and, similarly, springs too near the side of the seat will be covered by the stuffing in the arms.

As a guide for the height of the springs you will need, first measure the height of the ones you removed, then measure from the webbing up to the stuffing rail. These measurements should be about the same, if they are not, compromise. Springs of 10 swg (metal diameter) will usually be about right, but if the springs are very high, you should use 9 swg. Your chair will probably have three or four springs along the front edge, and across the centre, but it may have fewer in the back row. Space them evenly and face them so that the knot at the top of the spring is inwards. (If the knot faces outwards it will cut through the base hessian.) Mark around the springs with chalk then remove all but the one in the back left-hand corner. Thread the spring needle with heavy twine and, starting with a slip knot, sew the spring to the webbing in three places. As you replace each spring in position, face the knot inwards.

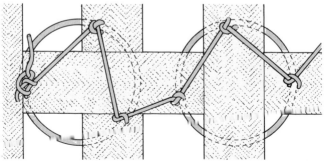

Attach each spring to the webbing in three places, beginning with a slip knot.

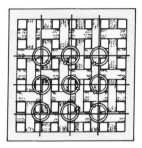

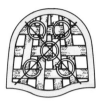

Spring patterns vary from chair to chair but the aim is always to distribute the springs evenly over the sitting area. Remember that most people move about on a chair – they don't sit in one spot the whole time.

Here a space has been left at the sides of the seat and at the back because the arms and back would otherwise protrude over the springs. After the springs have been sewn in position, they must be lashed to hold them in place.

Lashing (cording) springs

When you have attached all the springs to the webbing, they must be lashed together with laid cord. Start by placing pairs of 15mm (⅝in.) improved tacks on the top of the seat frame at opposite ends of each row of springs, leaving enough space between the frame and the tack head to take the laid cord. Bear in mind that, after they are lashed, the springs should be vertical but reduced in height by 2-2.5cm (¾-1in.). Leave about 30cm (12in.) at the end of the cord, then loop it round the tacks at one end and drive the tacks home. You need to put two half-hitches (one each side) of every spring. When you reach the other side of the frame, pull the

Lashing (cording) springs

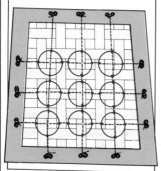

1 *Place pairs of tacks at both ends of each row of springs.*

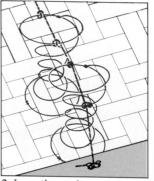

2 *Loop the cord round the tacks at one end.*

3 *Place a half-hitch on both sides of every spring.*

4 *Tie the loose ends up to the first and last springs.*

The bridle ties are inserted around the edge and to form a squared S shape over the centre of the seat.

cord tight around the tacks and drive the tacks home. Cut the cord about 30cm (12in.) from the tacks, then tie both loose ends back up to the outside springs. You have to repeat this process across each row of springs from side to side and back to front. When you have finished, the springs should all be straight but reduced in height by about 2cm (¾in.). If any of them look crooked, you will have to relash them.

First stuffing

Cover the springs with 340g (12oz.) base hessian, as described on pp. 18-19. Measure over the springs at the widest point and allow enough for handling. The hessian must be taut but make sure that it does not pull the springs down with it. Cut the hessian to fit around the back posts as described on p. 26. At the front corners, fold it back on itself from front to back and make a Y cut (see p. 39), level with the top outside edge of the front rail. Once the hessian is in place, stitch the springs to it in the same way as you stitched them to the webbing.

Insert bridle ties around the outer edge of the seat as described on pp. 20-1, but in the centre, work the ties in an S shape. They should all be about three fingers' high. Use fibre for the stuffing and tease it out and tuck it under the bridle ties as described on pp. 20-1. Put more around the outer edge and enough to form a thin cushion over the springs in the centre. Press down on the filling and if you can feel the springs, add more teased fibre, but keep in mind the finished height of the seat and do not make this first stuffing too high.

Stitching the seat

Cover the fibre with scrim and insert stuffing ties as described on pp. 26-7. Be careful here that you only put the point of the needle through the base hessian (the twine must not go through the webbing). If you pull the twine too far down into the spring area it will get caught up around the springs and laid cord. The scrim should be tacked down as described on pp. 26-7. When you get to the front corners, fold the scrim as you did the base hessian and make a Y cut. The scrim should now fit around the front post. At the back and sides, tack the scrim on the top of the rail. The seat itself should fit snugly up to the stuffing rails.

You will need to make a hard edge (edge roll) at the front of the seat; the number of rows of stitching required will depend on the height of the seat at the front edge, but usually in this type of seat, you will need two rows of blind (sink) stitching and two top rows (roll stitch). The top roll should be quite plump unless you want a sharp edge to the chair. Work the stitching as described on pp. 28-9. When you have finished, tighten the stuffing ties slightly and knot off.

Second stuffing

Insert bridle ties around the edge of the seat and in the centre as you did for the first stuffing. This second stuffing should be hair, teased out and tucked under the bridle ties as described on pp. 20-1. If your seat was domed slightly, add more hair in the centre and graduate it to the outside edge of the seat. Measure over the widest parts of the seat and halfway down the face edge of the seat rails and cut the calico to these measurements. Fit the calico as described on pp. 30-1. Tack both the back and the front before you make a Y cut at the front corners, since once you have cut the calico, you cannot move it again. The cuts to fit the calico around the back posts are the same as described on pp. 30-1. At the back and the sides (under the arms), tack the calico on top of the rails, as you did the scrim.

On armchairs linter felt makes a better wadding than skin wadding because it gives a softer feel to the surface of the top cover. Cut the felt to cover the seat and the calico at the front and go under the bottom edge of the arms and back. Be careful handling this felt as it tends to pull apart easily. Place it over the calico, press the seat down to leave a space, and tuck it under the back and arms. If it goes lumpy, it is best to take it off and start again.

Top cover

Cut a rectangle of top cover, remembering to centre the pattern. At the back and sides, the top cover will be tacked on top of the rails as the calico was, so measure to here and add about 5cm (2in.) for handling. If there is no show-wood along the front edge of the seat rail, the cover will go under the front rail and be tacked on the underside of the chair, so allow about 5cm (2in.) at this edge to go under the chair. Attach the top cover as described on pp. 30-1. At the front legs, place a pin at the corner of the leg and rail, then cut the cover upwards to the pin. Cut off the excess fabric and turn it under, then fold and tack it under the bottom of the chair and across the top of the leg. Drive the tacks home along the sides then fold the top cover inwards on top of itself and tack it home using 12mm (½in.) fine tacks. Trim off any excess fabric.

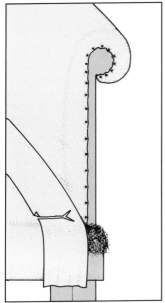

1 *Make Y cuts in both scrim and calico to fit around the rails.*

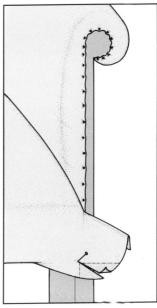

2 *Place a pin at the corner of the leg and rail; cut the cover to the pin.*

Scroll arms

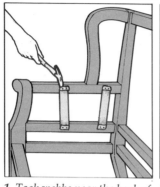

1 Tack webbs near the back of the arm and halfway along it.

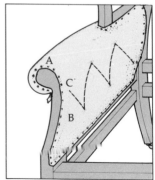

2 Tack webbing from the wing to the top of the front post.

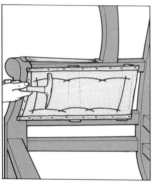

3 Fold the hessian round the webbing and insert bridle ties.

4 Tuck fibre under the webbing and fit the scrim.

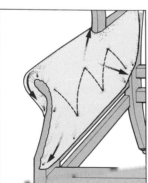

5 Tension the scrim to create a cigar shape.

6 Tack and smooth the scrim around the scroll.

Scroll arms

Fold a strip of webbing in half across its width and tack it as described on pp. 18-19 on the inside of the arm, about 5cm (2in.) in from the back post. Tack a full-width webb about halfway along the arm. Both need only be hand tight. Tack a rectangle of 340g (12oz.) base hessian as described on pp. 18-19 over the top of the arm rail to the stuffing rail, and from the front post to the back post. At the back, nick it top and bottom so that it folds around the back strip of webbing.

Insert bridle ties round the hessian, about 7.5cm (3in.) from the edge. Tack a piece of webbing on top of the arm rail close to the wing. Hand strain it over the top of the front post and tack it on top of the post. Prepare the first stuffing as described on pp. 26-7. Tuck plenty of fibre under the webbing on top of the arm rail, then fill the bridle ties. Cut a rectangle of scrim to fit from the outside of the stuffing rail, under the rail, over the filling and round to the outside of the arm, and from the back post, over the filling to the front of the front post (the facing), and add 5cm (2in.) on all sides for handling. Temporary tack it on the outside of the stuffing rail, the underside of the arm rail and at the centre of the facing. Remove the original temporary tacks if necessary, and tension. Re-temporary tack along the outside of the stuffing rail and under the arm rail, and put two or three tacks down the front of the facing.

Put stuffing ties in a zigzag pattern along the arm. Tuck the scrim under the fibre as described on pp. 26-7, and tack on the chamfered (beveled) edge. Work the top of the scroll (the scroll is the curve at the top of the facing) first (A), then do about halfway down the front edge (B), and go back and fill in the space between (C). Do not make pleats down the facing, the scrim should be smooth but protrude beyond the facing. To finish the underarm, add more filling and tuck the scrim under the fibre. Tack the scrim low on the outside of the arm rail up to the wing rail. To finish the point of the scroll, cut off the excess scrim, tuck it under and tack. Complete the rest of the scroll and drive all the tacks home around the front facing.

To fit the scrim around the wing rail, fold it back on itself and make a long Y cut in to the wing rail. Fold it to fit around the rail, adding more fibre if you need to. Make Y cuts so that the scrim passes through and under the arm, and tuck this 'tongue' around the webbing.

Stitching the scroll

The next stage is to regulate and stitch the scroll. Use the regulator to help you work the fibre into the edge of the scroll so that it will be firm once you have stitched it. Work the blind stitch as described on pp. 28-9 all around the front of the arm. The blind row does not need to go right to the point of the scroll since there is very little fibre there. Work a row of top stitches around the scroll, tapering the row so that it begins (or ends) at the point. Regulate the fibre into the edge as you make the stitches and remember that the roll should protrude beyond the facing when you have finished.

Remove the temporary tacks on the stuffing rail and add more filling so that the bottom of the arm sits neatly on top of the seat. Tuck the scrim under the fibre in the usual way and tack it on the outside of the stuffing rail. Make any necessary adjustments to the wing area of the arm and drive all the tacks home. The only part of the scrim not now tacked should be the tongue which you tucked around the webbing at the back of the arm.

To keep the shape of the arm, you should work a row of 5cm (2in.) top stitches (see pp. 28-9) along the outside edge of the arm.

Make fairly tight bridle ties (as described on pp. 20-1) to hold the thin hair second stuffing. Remember when you are doing the second stuffing to fill any hollows made by the stuffing ties and the rows of stitching; you should not be able to detect them when the calico is fitted. The hair must not come over the roll at the front of the arm, but you should put a reasonable amount on this edge.

Cut a rectangle of calico large enough to cover the whole of the stuffed part of the arm with about 5cm (2in.) for handling and temporary tack as described on pp. 30-1. Pull it tight around the front of the scroll, and temporary tack on the outside of the stuffing rail and under the arm rail. Skewer (pin) the calico at the top of the scroll, smooth it over the front of the facing and temporary tack it in about three places. Make a cut in the calico, leave about 15mm (⅝in.) around the top of the scroll and trim off any excess.

Start at the top of the scroll, turn the calico under the hair and pin it. Work around the scroll, pinning as you go. Remember that the calico should be smooth and taut, so if it feels a bit loose, remove the temporary tacks and tension down the front of the facing again.

Shaping the arm

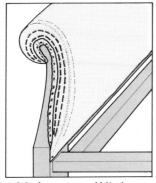

1 Work one row of blind stitches and one of top stitches.

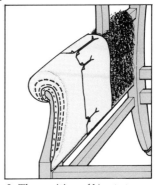

2 The position of Y cuts to fit scrim round rails.

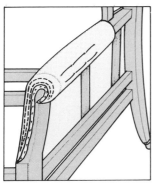

3 Make a row of top stitches on the outside edge.

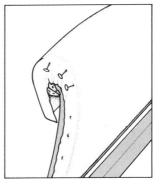

4 Skewer the calico at the top of the scroll.

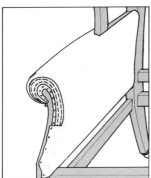

5 Turn the calico under the hair, then pin it.

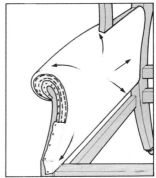

6 Tension the calico to keep the scroll shape as you go.

Finishing the scroll

At the back, remove the temporary tacks and fold the calico back, cutting it to fit around the wing rail, the arm rail and the stuffing rail, as you did the scrim, and re-temporary tack. Make a Y cut in the calico to fit around the front post and complete the tacking at the back, on the stuffing rail and under the arm rail. The calico should be quite tight – if it is loose it will make ugly wrinkles under the top cover – so when you are satisfied that it is taut in all directions, cut off all the excess. The calico pinned round the scroll must now be stitched in place. This is done with a knotted blanket stitch (sometimes called a joining stitch) and it is best to use slipping (buttoning) thread since this is less likely to show through the top cover. Work from where the calico was cut, round the top of the scroll to the point.

Use linter felt over the calico, ensuring that it covers all the stuffed part of the arm, but not the arm facing. Remember that it is far easier to pinch away excess than

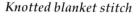

Knotted blanket stitch

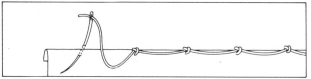

1 *Make knotted blanket stitches with slipping (buttoning) thread, since this is less likely to show through the top cover.*

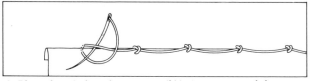

2 *Place the stitches about 10mm (³⁄₈in.) apart, round the scroll to the point.*

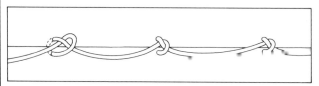

3 *Use the same stitch on a button-back chair (see pp. 68-9) to anchor the calico round the edge of the back.*

The first stuffing is enclosed with scrim to create the required shape and the second stuffing is covered with calico, tacked and stitched into place. A layer of wadding is placed over the calico and the top cover encases them all.

it is to add more without it looking lumpy. Cut a rectangle of top cover as you did for the calico. It must run down the inside of the arm and both arms must match as far as possible. The tacks should not go through the wadding so pinch the wadding away as necessary. Temporary tack the top cover as you did the calico; it must be quite tight. Smooth the cover over the front facing, temporary tack at the top of the scroll first and then divide the fabric into pleats all around the scroll. Face the pleats downwards towards the seat – they should appear to radiate from a point in the centre of the scroll. The top of the pleats should not go over the top of the arm. Tension and tack down the rest of the facing as you did the calico.

At the back of the arm, fold the cover as you did the calico and make Y cuts to fit around the wing rail, the arm rail and the stuffing rail. At the front, make a Y cut to fit around the front post. Tack off, adjust the tension as necessary, then trim off any excess fabric.

Sprung back

Springing a back is in many ways similar to springing a seat, so follow the basic instructions given on pp. 34-9.

Attach the horizontal webbs first, then fix the vertical webbs to the stuffing rail and tension them up to the top rail. If the springs that you removed from the back are in a reasonable condition, sort them into heights and place them on the webbing, with the taller ones nearest the seat. Face the knot part of the spring inwards. The springs should sit over the area where the webbs cross. Position, stitch them to the webbing and lash them in place as described on pp. 34-7, but make sure you do not strain them down, since this would make the back hard and unyielding. Fix 340g (12oz.) base hessian over the springs (see p. 37), cutting to fit around the arm rails. Do not overstrain the hessian. Sew the springs to the hessian as described on p. 37. Work around the outer edge of the back inserting the bridle ties, as described on pp. 20-1, then work some over the remainder of the back. They should all be about three fingers' high. Insert the first stuffing as described on p. 37, but put more at the bottom of the back to give some support to the sitter's lower back.

The scrim should be turned under and tacked on the front (top) surface of the back posts, on the outside of the stuffing rail at the bottom, and on the chamfered edge on the top rail. Temporary tack each side of the scrim first, then do the top rail, then the bottom. At the bottom, tuck it down between the seat and the fibre in the back.

Insert stuffing ties as described on pp. 26-7. The lower ones should be just below the top of the arms, so that the lumber support is free from ties. Avoid the springs and cords when you are inserting the ties. Remove the temporary tacks from the top rail, add more fibre, tuck the scrim under the filling and tack it on to the chamfered edge, as described on pp. 26-7. Work to within 5cm (2in.) of the sides, then fold the scrim back down the sides and make Y cuts to fit it around the top rail, the arm rail and stuffing rail. Complete the tacking on the top rail right up to the wings. Do the sides in the same way, then do the stuffing rail.

Make a row of blind stitches (see pp. 28-9) along the top edge of the back from post to post. Regulate the filling into the edge, then form a row of top stitching (see pp. 28-9). Tighten the stuffing ties slightly, and drive all

Springs in the back of a chair are placed where the webbs cross (left); in the back, they do not add shape (right), merely comfort.

the tacks fully home. The second stuffing of the back is put on as the seat was done, so follow the directions on pp. 38-9. Cut a rectangle of calico long enough to be tacked from the outside of the stuffing rail to the outside of the top rail, and wide enough to be tacked near the edge of the back posts. Tuck it down between the seat and the stuffing of the back and temporary tack it on the stuffing rail. Tension it up and over the hair, and temporary tack it on the outside of the back rail. If the calico is tight enough, it will not have to be retacked so fold it back down each side and make Y cuts to fit around the top, arm and stuffing rails. Smooth it back into place and tack it in its final position. Tension it up and out towards the corners, folding it under and angling it out. Form a mitre across the top of the back post at each corner.

When the tension is correct, hammer all the tacks home and trim off the excess calico.

Cover the whole of the back with linter felt, pinching away the excess around the arm and wing rails. At the top edge, the felt should not go over on to the outside back of the chair. Cut the top cover as you did the calico, but remember to centre any pattern. Place the cover on the wadding and temporary tack. Fold it down the sides as you did the calico and make Y cuts to fit around all the rails. Smooth it back into place and tack. Test for tension in both directions, and, when you are satisfied, drive the tacks home and trim off any excess fabric.

Wings

Tack a strip of webbing to the top of the arm at the back of the wing parallel to the back post, strain it up to the top of the wing rail, and tack it off on the inside. Tack a rectangle of 340g (12oz.) hessian on the inside of the wing; allow enough to enable you to tack it off on the inside of the back post. Tack it on the top of the arm, strain it upwards and tack it to the inside of the wing. Fold it back on itself, tack it again, then cut off any excess. Insert bridle ties as described on pp. 20-1.

Fill the inside wing with hair, putting more where it meets the inside back. Cut a rectangle of calico large enough to be tacked on the back posts, to come over the hair and be tacked on the outside of the wing rails. At the bottom, it should fold under the hair and sit neatly on top of the arm; the hair must not come over the edge of the rails here. At the back, fold the calico back parallel to the back post and make a Y cut (see p. 39) so that it fits around the top rail. Temporary tack the calico to the back post from the outside, then strain it to the front and temporary tack on the outsides of the wing rail and the top rail. There will be quite a lot of fullness around the curve of the wing but you can get rid of this by straining the calico out between the two sections you have already tacked. Drive all the tacks, except those down the back post, fully home.

Most wings are simple in construction; webbing and hessian support the filling, and the shape is created by the calico – rather like the drop-in seat.

Wings

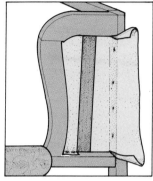

1 *The position of webbing and hessian on a wing.*

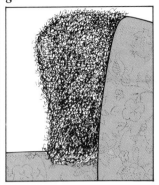

2 *Fill the inside wing with hair.*

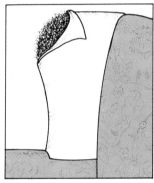

3 *Strain and smooth calico to create the shape.*

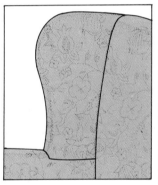

4 *Press all the fillings inwards down the back post.*

Use skin wadding over the calico, pinching away the excess as necessary, and tuck it under the wing where it sits on the arm. Cut a rectangle of top cover the same size as you cut the calico, and place it over the wadding. Tuck it under the wing to sit on the arm, and temporary tack it on the back post. Strain it over the wing and temporary tack on the outside of the rail as you did the calico. Make Y cuts to fit it around the top rail. Fold it to form a mitre across the top of the back post and to join up to the inside back cover. Press all the layers and filling inwards down the back post so that the back of the wing sits neatly up to the inside back and tack through all the thicknesses. Fold all the thicknesses inwards and add two or three more tacks.

Outside covers

Cut a rectangle of base hessian to cover from under the arm down to the bottom of the chair (it does not need to go under the chair), and from the back post to the front post of the arm. Cut the top cover as for the hessian but allow enough to go under the chair and around the back and front posts by about 5cm (2in.).

With the chair on its side, place the top cover on the outside of the arm, fold the top edge under the arm, and pin it at the back and the front along the fold line. Gently lift the cover and hang it over the arm. Fix it in place with two or three tacks under the arm rail. Position the hessian over the top cover and fix that

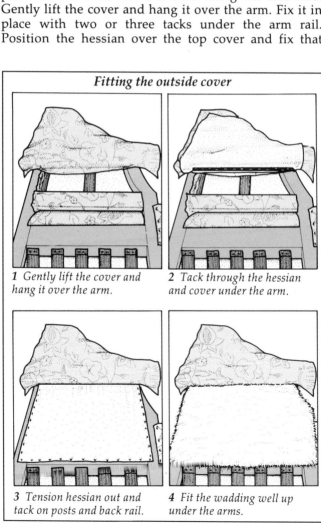

Fitting the outside cover

1 Gently lift the cover and hang it over the arm.

2 Tack through the hessian and cover under the arm.

3 Tension hessian out and tack on posts and back rail.

4 Fit the wadding well up under the arms.

under the arm with two or three tacks. Use a length of back tacking strip and tack through the hessian and top cover underneath the arm. Make sure that the tacking strip is in line with the outside of the chair.

Fold the hessian down flat on the side of the chair, tension it out and tack on the posts and bottom rail. Leave it raw at the edges, but cut off any excess. Place a sheet of skin wadding over the hessian, making sure it fits well up under the arms. Fold the cover carefully over the wadding so as not to disturb it. Make sure the cover is square, then temporary tack it underneath the chair, on the back of the back post and on the front facing. Cut it to fit around the legs of the chair as described on pp. 30-1.

Cut a rectangle of top cover large enough to cover the facing easily, and ensure that it is square. Use some linter felt to pad out the facing, then lay the cover over it. Trim off any excess, but leave enough to tuck under the wadding – about 12mm (½in.) should be sufficient. Starting at the top of the scroll, tuck the cover under the wadding and pin it up to the edge. Work all round the facing, including the bottom, in this way. You will have to snip the cover at the point of the scroll, but be careful not to snip too much. When this is all pinned in place, slip-stitch the facing to the cover, using slipping thread and a curved needle. Work all around the facing, making two or three stitches, then pulling them gently to close up the seam. Remove the pins as you work.

Tack a piece of hessian over the wing area. Leave the edges raw and trim off any excess. Cut a rectangle of top cover large enough to cover the outside wing and to turn under at the edge and along the bottom. Pin the cover to the edge and slip-stitch it in place all around the wing. Tack it off on the outside of the back post.

Cut a rectangle of hessian to cover the chair back and tack in place, then place skin wadding over it. Cut a rectangle of top cover large enough to cover the outside back, allowing enough to turn under the wadding along the top and down the sides, and to be tacked under the bottom of the chair. Place the cover over the wadding and, starting at the top rail, turn the edge under the wadding, pinning it in place as you work. Pin down each side and cut to fit around the legs at the bottom as described on pp. 30-1. Tack under the bottom of the chair and then slip-stitch it in place.

Finally, put on a bottom covering to keep in the dust; follow the directions given on pp. 22-3.

Project 4: Sofa with cushioned seat

Basic construction

Although the arms and the back on a sofa like this are very similar to those on a wing armchair, the seat construction is rather different. In addition to the main springs in the seat, there is also a row of springs along the front of the seat which move independently of the main springs. This front row of springs is fixed to the top of the front rail and does not sit on webbing. All the springs are individually lashed (corded) but then a cane or wire is lashed to them so that, to some extent, they move together; the cane forms a straight line along the front of the seat. The finished appearance of the seat is flat over the main area but a lip is formed along the front (over the front edge springs) to help prevent the cushions from slipping forward.

The other major difference between this and the other projects is the addition of cushions, in this case, piped box border cushions. Although foam- or polyester-filled cushions are acceptable, feather cushions are the most suitable although they do need plumping up after use.

Although it is not essential to fit collars to the inside back over the arms section, if you want the sofa to look really professional, take the time to fit them. They enable you to tailor the sections of upholstery much more cleanly than you would otherwise be able to. Practise the technique on old curtains or something similar before you start using the cover fabric. They can, of course, be fitted to a chair, if you need them.

Preparation

When you strip the sofa, make notes on the finishing, on the height of the seat with and without the cushions, and the depth of the seat from front to back.

The springs in the seat will probably not be usable but those in the back should be all right. The cane or wire along the front edge should be in a reasonable condition so keep this to reuse. Work the seat first because it will be easier without the arms and back covered in upholstery.

Left: *Re-upholstering a sofa with scroll arms and cushions will take a considerable amount of time, so set aside as many full days as you can. A skirt (top), which is made up in sections and slip-stitched to the main cover, is optional.*

Seat

Webb the seat as described on pp. 34-5, but in addition tack strips of webbing across the centre of the seat from back to front to give some support to the long webbs and prevent them sagging.

Calculate the required height of the springs as described on pp. 34-5 but remember that the front edge springs will be shorter than the main springs because they sit on the front rail. Make sure that you position the main springs so that the lashing cords will not interfere with the front edge springs.

Sew and lash the springs in place as described on pp. 34-7. If your springs are higher than 23cm (9in.), you will have to lash them through their centres *before* lashing them along the top. The method is exactly the same. When you have finished lashing, the springs should all be vertical and reduced in height by at least 25mm (1in.).

Left: *Position the main springs so that the lashing cords will not interfere with the front edge springs.*

Below: *Fold the twine in half and loop it around the bottom coil (bottom). Then, hold the spring at the correct height and make a clovehitch at both sides.*

When the twine is tacked to the front of the rail, the spring should be the correct height.

Front edge springs

Cut a length of webbing slightly longer than the full length of the rail and temporary tack this on top of the rail at each end. Slide the bottom coil of all the springs underneath the webbing, and hammer 15mm (⅝in.) improved tacks through the webbing on both sides of the coil. Cut a length of stout twine about six times the height of the spring and lash each spring individually to the height of the seat, as shown in the illustrations opposite.

Cut a length of stitching twine about 75cm (30in.) long, fold it in half and lash the springs to the cane or wire which you removed when stripping down the seat. Do this right along the front, keeping each spring upright, and on the side and back of the end springs if the cane reaches this far. Finally, put a row of tacks along the front edge of the frame and fix laid cord around the tacks and up to each spring, see below.

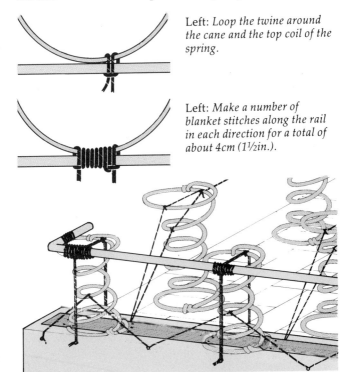

Left: *Loop the twine around the cane and the top coil of the spring.*

Left: *Make a number of blanket stitches along the rail in each direction for a total of about 4cm (1½in.).*

The final lashing of the springs will draw them forward so that the cane protrudes slightly beyond the seat rail.

First stuffing

Cover the springs with 340g (12oz.) hessian (burlap), as described on p. 37, but this time, make a gutter or well by tucking the hessian down between the main section of springs and the front edge springs. Cut a strip of webbing about 20cm (8in.) longer than the sofa. Fold it in half and lay it in the gutter. Temporary tack at one end using 15mm (⅝in.) tacks, strain it to the other end, and temporary tack there.

Tack the hessian in place as described on p. 37. Be careful not to displace the edge springs by pulling them down. At the ends of the edge springs, cut and fold the hessian as neatly as possible, remembering that the stuffing must not penetrate into the spring area. Sew the springs, including those along the front edge, to the hessian as described on p. 37.

Insert bridle ties (see pp. 20-1) with fine twine, forming lines of loops along the seat about 15cm (6in.) apart, and about three fingers' high. Fill the seat, the top of the edge springs and the gutter with fibre as described on pp. 26-7, but do not fill the front and sides of the edge spring area at this stage. Enclose the fibre with scrim as described on pp. 26-7. At the front edge, lay the scrim over the fibre and temporary tack along the sides and back. Tension the scrim over the front edge and skewer (pin) it to the hessian.

Insert stuffing ties over the main seat area as described on pp. 26-7 and put a separate row of ties along the gutter parallel with the front of the gutter (AB). With the stuffing ties in place, remove the skewers from the front edge and add more fibre if the edge feels soft. Tuck the scrim under the fibre and skewer it in place, making sure the skewer goes *under* the cane. Work along the front edge in this way. Form the corners into neat pleats. The process of tacking the scrim is as described on pp. 26-7, but this time it is skewered under the cane instead of being tacked to a wooden rail. With the front edge skewered in place, form a row of blind (sink) stitches as described on pp. 28-9, but pass the needle through the scrim and *under* the cane on the *upward* stroke and *over* the cane on the *downward* stroke.

Form a row of top stitches along the front edge section as described on pp. 28-9. Remember to regulate the fibre into the edge. In profile, the seat should now have a lip along its edge.

The front edge

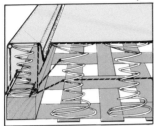

1 *Hold hessian in the gutter with webbing.*

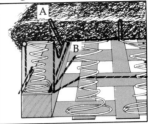

2 *Set stuffing ties in the gutter at the angle AB.*

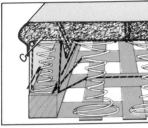

3 *Skewer the scrim under the cane.*

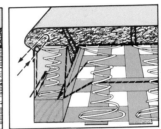

4 *Insert a row of blind stitches along the front edge.*

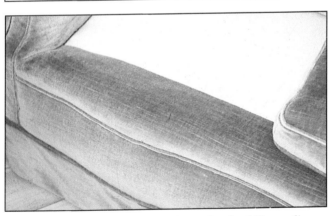

Keep in mind as you work that the front edge should have a lip to prevent the cushions slipping forward.

Tuck the scrim under and tack it home along the back and each side, adding more fibre as you go. Remember that the top of the seat should come to the stuffing rail, otherwise, in spite of the cushions, a gap will appear. Slightly tighten the stuffing ties and knot them off.

Second stuffing

Insert bridle ties (see pp. 20-1) to hold the second stuffing in place; make them about two fingers' high. Fill the main part of the seat, and stop just behind the gutter. Because the seat will have cushions, you do not need to put calico (muslin) over the second stuffing.

Cut a rectangle of top cover to fit over the spring edge from the gutter to the bottom of the lip. Use platform fabric to cover the main part of the seat from the gutter to the back rail, and allow 5cm (2in.) for handling. Machine sew the two sections of cover to a strip of webbing long enough to be tacked off on the seat rails and sewn to the seat. Put the right sides of the fabrics together with the webbing on top and sew.

Place the cover on the seat with the webbing at the back of the gutter. Tack the webbing to the seat rails at both ends ensuring that the line is parallel with the front of the sofa and sew the webbing to the seat scrim. Finish the second stuffing of the main part of the seat, and lay a piece of linter felt over the stuffing, ensuring that it fits well up to the machine line. Fold the platform section over the linter felt and temporary tack and fit it as described on pp. 38-9.

Second stuff the front lip of the seat and cover it with linter felt. Ease the cover over the lip and skewer it under the front edge. Form double pleats at the corners and skewer them in place. Secure a length of twine under the lip at one end, tension it along the front and secure it at the other end. Now stitch the cover along the edge. Use a curved needle and make a row of stitches 12mm (½in.) apart over the twine, through the cover and into the scrim.

Cut the front border wide enough to pass well into the sides between the seat and posts and deep enough to tack off on the underside of the seat rail, with 12mm (½in.) extra at the top edge. Make a strip of piping (see p. 75), long enough to be tacked off on the back of the front posts, and attach it to the top of the border. Place the border in position and fold the seam down along the top. Skewer it in place. Pass the ends through to the inside of the seat and tack off the piping on the back of the front posts. Slip-stitch the border along the top edge. Fold the border back and pad the front section lightly, then fold the material down and smooth it into place. Tack it off on the bottom of the seat rail. Fold and tack off the lower section on to the bottom of the rail.

Fitting the top cover

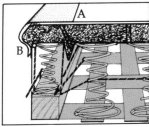

1 The top cover fits over the lip from A to B.

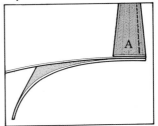

2 Sew the platform and lip section to the webbing at A.

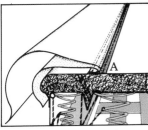

3 Sew the webbing to the scrim at A.

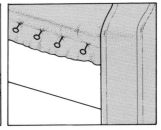

4 Skewer the fabric to hold it in place.

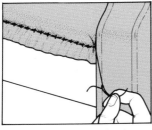

5 Tension a length of twine under the lip and stitch.

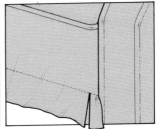

6 The border fits between the seat and front post.

Arms

Like the wing armchair, the sofa has scroll arms and the method of construction is essentially the same. You should, therefore, follow the general directions given on pp. 40-5. The calico and top cover material on a sofa, however, are taken to the back of the arms and tacked off on the back of the back post. Similarly, the filling is taken to the back of the arms.

This is a typical scroll arm.

Back

Construct the back as described on pp. 46-7 but continue the tacking off of the scrim and the stitching over the corners and down the sides of the back to finish at the arms. Cut the scrim and the calico to fit around the back posts and the arms.

Position a rectangle of fabric over the inside back where it will eventually fit, and cut off any excess around the arm. Leave about 12mm (½in.) for a seam. Cut a straight strip of fabric wide enough to pass over the arm and be tacked on the back post and long enough to fit right round the shape of the arm; this also needs a 12mm (½in.) seam allowance. Sew the collar piece around the curve of the inside back. Re-place it on the chair and temporary tack on the stuffing rail at the bottom and on the outside of the top rail. Make Y cuts in the collar to fit it around the rails and tack home. Complete tacking the fabric to the outside back. At the top corners, make pleats in the fabric. Face them either all to the centre or out and down towards the arms.

Fit the outside arms, back, facings and bottoming as described on pp. 50-1.

Cushions

Feather cushions are the most satisfactory and not expensive to have made professionally. Make a pattern or template for each cushion and have the inner cases made by a cushion-maker.

Making a collar

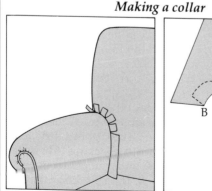

1 Lay fabric on chair back and snip to fit around arm.

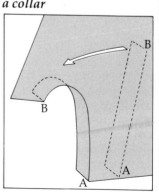

2 Sew collar strip to inside back from A to B.

Either platform fabric or top cover material can be used for the part of the seat under the cushions. The cushions are piped box border cushions; sew the borders together at the corners (left) and attach them to the platform.

Lay out the top cover and place the templates on the fabric, which should run from the back to the front of the seat. Add about 12mm (½in.) seam allowance all around the templates. Cut a top and bottom (called platforms) for each cushion. The sides (borders) are cut as five separate pieces – one for the front and each side and two for the back which contains the zip. Assemble the zip section first, then join the four borders together and check that they fit the platforms. The seams in the borders must exactly meet the corners of the platforms. Make up the piping (see p. 75) directly on the platform, starting part way along the back edge.

Partly open the zip and pin the seams of the borders to the corners of the platforms. The upper fabric tends to walk away as you sew, so keep checking that border and platform are aligned. Sew with the platform on the machine bed and the border on top. If when you have finished the borders are a little away from the piping, sew around the corners again with the border on the machine bed and the platform on top.

Project 5: Nineteenth-century button-back nursing chair

Basic construction

The major difference between this and the previous projects is in the construction of the back. Here, a roll of stuffing around the edge of the inside back is created, leaving a space in the centre. Calico (muslin) is anchored at the points where you will put the buttons and is stuffed to give it shape. The calico is then covered with wadding (batting), and the top cover is fixed in place by the buttons in the centre section and by tacking around the outer edge to just inside the show-wood line. The area for tacking is usually very narrow and close to the show-wood in this type of chair and you must take care not to split the wood at this point. Use smaller tacks, and, if possible, fewer of them than usual. Slip-stitching the outer covers in place is not possible here. The outside back has to be fixed to the wood with tacks which are covered with gimp or braid. Glue this in place in the usual way, but be careful on the inside back as there is very little space and it is easy to get the adhesive on the top cover.

Preparation

It is vital to make notes when you are stripping down a buttoned chair, and it will help if you keep the top cover for the pattern of the buttoning, and to enable you to make a rough calculation of the top covering. Before you remove the base hessian (burlap) from the back of the chair, measure the distance between the twines used to hold the buttons in place. Make a diagram of the pattern and the distances between the buttons from the centre of the chair. With this type of chair, you will have to work the back first; it is far more difficult to do both the back and the small sections each side of the back, rather like very low arms, when the seat is in position.

Choose your top cover fabric carefully. Buttoning will send stripes crooked, and a very large pattern is lost in the buttoning. An all-over pattern of small or medium size is usually acceptable, but avoid glazed cottons – they are rather stiff and are not easy to work into pleats. Unglazed cottons work very well

Left: This chair is a good choice for a first buttoning project because the buttoning is fairly simple. The construction of the back is different from the pieces discussed so far, but all the other techniques involved are familiar from previous projects.

Back

Place two strips of webbing (see pp. 18-19) on the inside of the back of the chair. Tack them to the stuffing rail at the bottom, then hand tension them to the top of the chair. Leave as much space as possible between the show-wood and the edge of the webbing.

Cut a rectangle of 340g (12oz.) hessian large enough to cover the inside back area. Leaving as much space as possible between the tacks and the show-wood, temporary tack it on to the stuffing rail, then tension it to the top. Keep the tension vertical to retain the curve of the chair. If the horizontal tension is too great, the back will be very flat when you have finished. Tack all around the back, cut off the excess, fold the hessian over and tack it back on itself (see pp. 18-19). Mark a line down the centre of the back.

Cut a rectangle of scrim about 18cm (7in.) larger all round than the base hessian, fold it in half and mark a vertical centre line. Skewer (pin) the scrim to the base hessian, matching the centre lines, then secure it with a running stitch 9cm (3½in.) inside the show-wood. Stitch it along the bottom of the chair about 16cm (6in.) up from the stuffing rail. Use a curved needle and fine twine and make small stitches.

Place the chair on its back and support it with pieces of padded wood to prevent damage to the show-wood. Start in the centre top, and stuff teased fibre under the scrim; turn the scrim under the fibre (see pp. 26-7) and temporary tack it in place. This roll needs to be firm and to follow the line of the frame. Work the top centre section first, then do the middle of the sides and then fill in the gaps between. Trim the excess scrim away as you work, so that you reduce the amount that has to be turned under.

At the bottom, fill the lumber region well to give support to the sitter. This part should also sit neatly on the seat when the chair is completed so keep this in mind as you work. When you are satisfied with the shape, drive all the tacks home.

Stitch around the edge roll so that it holds its shape. Use a fairly large curved needle in place of the usual bayonet needle, and if you can get a double-ended one, the stitching will be quite easy. (Filing a point on the eye end of a large curved needle will help if you can't.) Form a row of blind (sink) stitches (see pp. 28-9) very close to the tacks all around the edge but not along the bottom, then form a row of top stitches (see pp. 28-9) above the blind row, remembering to regulate the fibre into the edge as you work. The roll should now be wedge-shaped.

When the wedge-shaped edge roll is complete, you have the basic shape of the back. The stuffing under the calico and the final buttoning are all within this edge, although the outer pleats are tacked to the frame.

Making a buttoning plan

Marking out the button pattern can be confusing, so plan it out on a sheet of paper, using the measurements you took between the twines on the base hessian when you were stripping down. Remember that the diamonds should be equally spaced and taller than they are wide.

Place a tack on the centre line where the bottom row of buttons will be. From this point measure half the width of the diamond each side of the line and place tacks at these points (A). Now measure up from these tacks the full height of the diamonds (B). From the original tack measure up half the height of a diamond (C). Make sure that the distance from the centre line at B is the same as at A. Continue measuring the button points and placing tacks in the scrim, ensuring that both the horizontal and vertical lines run parallel. None of the tacks on the outside should be closer to the show-wood than half the size of the diamond. If the pattern of diamonds formed by the tacks looks too close to the edge at some points, adjust the diamonds until they look acceptable. Check that you have the number of rows and lines correct by referring to the original top cover. The distances between the buttons marked on the top cover will be up to 4cm (1½in.) longer than on the base hessian, to allow for the filling. When you are satisfied that the tacks are in the right position, remove each one in turn and mark its position carefully with a permanent marker.

Mark out the calico (the top cover will have the same markings so note the button distances). To calculate how much calico you need, measure over the edge roll at the widest point and add 3.5cm (1⅜in.) for each button; if, for example, the width is 60cm (23½in.) and there are three buttons at the widest point, the calico should measure 60cm + 10.5cm = 70.5cm (23½in. + 4⅛in. = 27⅝in.) total width. Calculate the length in the same way, measuring from the outside of the stuffing rail.

Fold the calico in half vertically to find the centre and mark it with tailor's chalk. Mark the position of the bottom row of buttons (A). To find this line, measure from the stuffing rail up to the bottom buttons. Strike two lines (B and C), each the full height of the diamond, plus the 3.5cm (1⅜in.) allowance, for example 13cm + 3.5cm = 16.5cm (5in. + 1⅜in. = 6⅜in.) On line A measure out from the centre line half the width of the diamond – including the 3.5cm (1⅜in.) allowance, for example 10cm + 3.5cm halved = 6.75cm (4in. + 1⅜in. = 5⅜in. halved = 2¹¹⁄₁₆in.) – on both sides and mark these points (D). Repeat at lines B and C (the height of one and two diamonds) and mark points E and F. From points D, E and F, measure and mark the full width of the diamond, i.e. 13.5cm (5⅜in.); this will give you points G, H and J. Join these points up diagonally; the points where the lines cross give you the other button points. Mark only the points that will have buttons with coloured chalk.

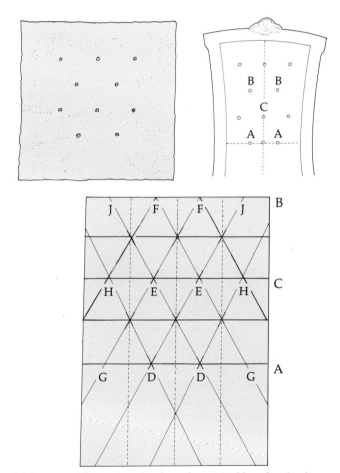

Make a rough buttoning plan from the original base hessian (top left), then mark out the button pattern on the chair with tacks (top right). The points that will actually be buttoned should be marked on both the calico and the top cover with coloured tailor's chalk.

Attaching buttons

Cut lengths of twine about 30cm (12in.) long, thread a buttoning needle and stab through the calico, scrim and base hessian, slightly to one side of the first button point. Pull this end of the twine through, rethread the needle with the other end of the twine and stab through on the other side of the button point. Form a slip knot with these two ends to hold the calico firmly in place. Place a small 'butterfly' of calico or wadding under the twine loop to stop it tearing the calico. Repeat this at all the button position(s) on the bottom row, then do the next row up.

Tease some hair and tuck it under the calico to pad out between the button points. Add more hair *underneath* the first handful. The calico should form diagonal pleats between the button points. Ease these into place as you put in more filling, making sure there are no hollows under them. When you have filled the gaps between the first two rows of buttons, do the third row and fill that, and so on until you have worked the centre of the chair. Then work round the outside, so that the whole of the back is full and level with the top of the edge roll.

Skewer the calico all round the edge. Cut off the excess, tuck it under the hair and pin it slightly over the edge of the roll. Fold the pleats in place on the edge, then work a knotted blanket stitch as on the scroll arm to hold the calico in position (see pp. 44-5). At the bottom, add more hair over the scrim and tack the calico on the outside of the stuffing rail. Fold the pleats straight down from the bottom buttons.

Cut a rectangle of top cover a little larger than you cut the calico and mark out the button pattern with tailor's chalk on the *back* of the cover.

Cut a piece of linter felt to cover the whole of the chair back and place it over the calico. Carefully make holes in the felt by gently easing it apart at the button points on the bottom row. Position the top cover. Insert the twine through the top cover but this time thread a button on to the twine before you stab back through. Ease the button down into the hole in the felt and pull the twine taut. Make a slip knot on the back and insert a butterfly of fabric or webbing between the hessian and the knot. Use the regulator to ease the pleats, which should face down towards the seat, into place. When all the buttons are in place, tighten the twines and tie them

Attaching buttons

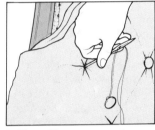

1 Place a butterfly under the twine loop.

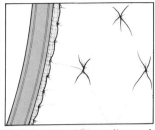

2 Calico should form diagonal pleats between button points.

3 Thread buttons on twine; knot twine at the back.

4 Use the regulator to ease pleats into place.

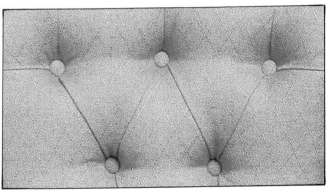

The buttons should be pulled down evenly and the pleats form as near perfect diamond shapes as possible.

off. Fold the pleats at the top and sides into place and tack off. The side pleats should all face down but the top and bottom ones can face either in or out. Temporary tack the bottom on to the outside of the stuffing rail, and leave it like this until the seat is complete. Cut off the excess fabric.

Side sections

The small section each side of the seat, where the back curves around it, should be completed before you start the seat. Tack a small piece of top cover quite close to the show-wood. Pad it with linter felt and ensure that it lines up with the bottom part of the back. Tack it off below the line of the seat.

Seat

Fix the webbing, springs and base hessian as described on pp. 34-7. Apply the fibre filling, tack down the scrim and work the stitching as described on pp. 28-9, and follow the directions given on pp. 30-1 for the front corners. Attach the second stuffing, calico, linter felt and top cover as described on pp. 29-31, but take the top cover under the seat rails and tack it on the bottom of the chair. At the back, tack off the top cover on the top of the seat rails.

Outside covers

Work this step with the chair facing down. Draw a line in chalk around the back of the chair where the cover will finish – this may already be marked out but they are frequently lopsided. Tack a piece of 340g (12oz.) hessian in place over the whole of the back using 10mm (⅜in.) fine tacks. Cut off the excess up to the tacks.

Place a piece of skin wadding over the hessian. Lay the top cover in place and, making sure it is straight, temporary tack it at the top, bottom and the sides. Start in the centre of the top and turn the cover under so that the fold is level with the chalk line. Trim off the excess and tack home. Work all around the back curve in this way. At the bottom, cut the cover to fit around the legs and tack off under the seat rail.

If the side sections are short, take the cover around the back in one piece. If they are rather long, you will have to cover them separately. Treat them as small versions of the back but where they meet the back make a neat fold; alternatively, machine stitch them. Lay the top cover fabric on the back of the chair, pin, then machine, the extra pieces in place, and then tack permanently, as described above. Finish all the edges with gimp (see pp. 31 and 74-5).

Fix the bottoming as described on pp. 22-3.

Once the techniques of buttoning have been mastered, there is no reason why you should not attempt more complicated buttoning projects.

Fabrics for upholstery

There are so many types of fabric available for upholstered furniture that it is impossible here to give anything more than a rough guide. The yarn used in upholstery fabrics is strong to withstand hard wear, and usually closely woven. Fabrics can be made from natural and man-made materials (fibres) or a combination of both. A good supplier can advise you on the fibre content and quality.

In Britain, many fabrics conform to a fire retardancy code. Natural fibres tend to be more absorbent than man-made, which could be important if you will be sitting in the chair for long periods at a time. The feel of the fabric is also important – some tweed fabrics, for example, can be uncomfortable because they 'scratch' through thin clothing.

When you first start, it is better to keep to fabrics with a fairly plain weave and finish; weaves like twill can be difficult to work with. Stretch fabrics are usually knitted, although some are woven and have the elastic thread woven into them. As a general rule, knitted fabrics are not easy to handle and tend to lose their shape in time. Avoid fabrics with a shiny surface until you are experienced – they tend to allow any pull marks (called tack ties) where the tacks are inserted.

Glazed cottons are fine for simple surfaces such as drop-in seats, but because they are stiff, they do not ease around difficult shapes. Stripes can be difficult to work with because the tension needs to be kept along the line of the stripe rather than from side to side.

There are many fabrics suitable for upholstery, but you should always take into account the texture, in addition to the colour and the pattern, when you are choosing.

Above all, try to choose a fabric suitable for the piece of furniture; a large pattern, for example, will not look good on a small chair.

Estimating fabric for a chair

To estimate the quantity of fabric required for a chair, measure each section (seat, inside back, inside arm, outside back, outside arm, facings), and list them with the width of each section first. You can measure over the old upholstery before you strip the chair, but take into account (a) that the stuffing (filling) will have collapsed a little, particularly in the seat, and (b) that you may not build the upholstery back to exactly the same size and shape as the original. Remember when you are measuring that in most cases each piece will be tacked off on a hidden rail, so you will also need some extra for handling. From your list of measurements, make up a cutting plan (see p. 76). Juggle the sections around to get the most economical plan and remember that the pattern has to run in the same direction.

Although it is better to cut piping (welting) on the true bias, unless you have very sharp corners to work you can cut it on the straight grain. Piping and facings can be cut from the spare fabric alongside the main sections.

Upholstery trimmings

Trimmings for upholstered furniture are more than simply decorative; they hide tack heads, cover raw edges and hide joins in the fabric.

Tack heads and raw edges are easily covered with gimp or braid. You can either sew this on, fix it with gimp pins or glue it in place with a clear adhesive (see p. 31). Gimp is available in many designs and colours, and it is also possible to have gimp specially dyed if necessary. Although fringe is not much used for furniture these days, some period furniture looks good with heavy fringe fixed around the bottom of the seat.

Decorative nails are available in many designs and sizes in brass or bronze and can be close nailed, without spaces, or spaced. If you intend to use nails, use fewer tacks to hold the top cover, so that there are spaces for them. They are not the easiest of finishes to apply, because some upholstery nails tend to buckle when they are struck. One way of preventing this is to make a hole with a nail or similar sharp object so that you do not have to use too much force when you are driving in the upholstery nail.

Decorative cord is available in many colours and thicknesses and can be slip-stitched in position. Do not glue cord. Piping or welting is often inserted into the seams of cushions, but it can be used anywhere where there is a seam – the seam allowance has to be hidden. You can slip-stitch it in place to the outside of a chair cover, and then sew the outside cover and the piping to the main cover in one operation.

Another seam finish which can be used in the same way as piping is ruche. You can buy this ready made. Like piping, it has a seam allowance for sewing. It is rather bulky, so its use is somewhat limited.

If you have an old piece of furniture which did not have its original upholstery and you are unsure of what trimming you should use, do some research. Look at reference books on furniture (not all are accurate, so look at several). Many museums have libraries which are open to the public, or ask the furniture department of your museum for advice.

Gimp and braid can be difficult to colour match to fabric, so match the gimp to a fabric sample before you buy it.

Piping (welting)

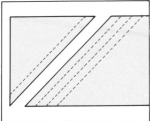

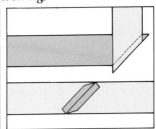

1 Cut crosswise strips 40mm (1½in.) wide.

2 Join the piping and trim the seams to 15mm (⅝in.).

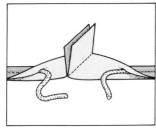

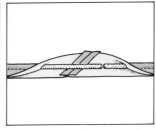

3 Stitch the cord into the strips of fabric.

4 Join the cord by oversewing a few times.

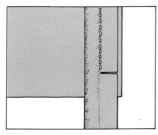

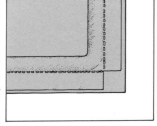

5 When you insert piping, at corners, leave the needle down, lift the foot, snip the piping, turn, lower the foot and continue.

Cutting plans

Plan A is for 120cm (48in.) wide fabric and plan B is for 140cm (55in.) wide fabric. Many fabrics are now made to this wider measure, so check this before you buy. If your chosen fabric has a pattern, you will need extra material for matching. To calculate how much, for every second line across your cutting plan, add the length of the pattern repeat once: plan A, therefore, requires 3 pattern repeats extra, and plan B requires 2½ pattern repeats extra.

List of measurements taken from the chair

	width	length
S(seat)	120cm (47in.)	100cm (39½in.)
I/B (inside back)	85cm (33½in.)	100cm (39½in.)
I/A (inside arm)	75cm (29½in.)	60cm (23½in.)
O/B (outside back)	63cm (25in.)	75cm (29½in.)
O/A (outside arm)	70cm (27½in.)	40cm (16in.)
F (facings)	10cm (4in.)	25cm (10in.)

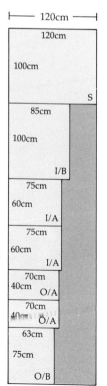

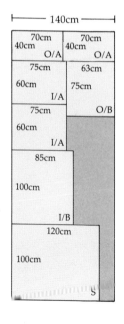